songs
of solace & sorrow
a pandemic journey

David MacGregor

Published by
David MacGregor
with the assistance of lulu.com
© 2020
all music score © David MacGregor – Willow Publishing
Images from lightstock.com, unsplash.com *and* pixabay.com used with permission.

Permission is granted to use and copy portions from this book in not for profit settings without contacting the author.

For all commercial publication permissions, please contact David MacGregor

First printed December 2020

Creator:	MacGregor, David
Title:	Songs of solace and sorrow
ISBN:	978-0-646-82747-6
	Imprint: David MacGregor

9 780646 827476

Subjects:	Instrumental piano pieces
	Worship songs
	Reflections

Contents

- titles in italics are piano instrumentals

Foreword … Craig Mitchell	4
Songs … an introduction	5
I'll Hold You Forever	6
We've Lit a Candle	8
Fall	11
Presence	15
The Long Road	19
Be Still	22
Resilience	25
Sacrifice	29
Awaken	31
Crazy!	33
Agitated	37
We Will Remember Them	39
Emerging	43
Fasing	47
Stitch a New Garment	50
Perspective	53
Liminal	55
Your Love Will Follow	57
Make It Joyful!	59
Image of Love	64
Lord, How We Thank You	68
Loss	71
Gathering Stones Together	73
Emptying	75
Dear COVID	77

Foreword ...Craig Mitchell

It starts with a piano.
Not with praise, but with poignancy. Not with words, but with the melody of melancholy.

We all know moments of heavy sadness - the pain of grief, the length of loss, when prayer is difficult and gratitude impossible. At such times, the closeness of community can seem a gift or a grind. Sorrow craves solitude, for a time. Solace seeks company. So what happens when isolation is interminable? When the global pandemic flooded us in early 2020, everything went quiet. We contracted into our lockdown lives, our emotional shells. However, the usually creative David Macgregor suddenly began a productive streak that went on and on, and then on some more! He kept posting new music online. People began to say, "This is expressing how I'm feeling right now." Ministers said, "Can I use this in worship on Sunday?"

David's music is characteristically singable and memorable. It is also, most importantly, prayerful. Many of his songs are expressions of the heart in worship, telling of God's grace toward us and of our seeking to follow Christ. Encounter and response. The best worship music somehow meets us in the moment and also takes us somewhere. We are moved within ourselves and also beyond ourselves into God's bigger picture for our world.

What surprised others and even David himself were the instrumentals given birth these past months. Here he is at the piano, digging deep to express the spirit journey of solitude, struggle and searching that we all found ourselves journeying through. No easy answers. No simple chorus. A season of loss and lament. A twilight of longing, and yet also a coming glimpse of sunrise. A new song in the dawning.

David's music has been sung for decades in local churches, at camps and retreats, in significant regional church gatherings. He has written memorable theme songs for Synod and Assembly meetings. I've played his songs many, many times. He is no doubt the most prolific and probably the most widely known songwriter in the Uniting Church in Australia.

However, this collection of songs are not big event songs. These songs are for solitude and retreat, and for the coming together of people who feel the need to gather, even when they cannot. They are an invitation to take time to wait, to dwell in uncertainty, to know our longing - both for God and for our own human wholeness. Some songs need space, so give these some space in worship. Both despair and healing need time.

For the Christian community, there is also the promise of grace, even when we the travel through a shadowed valley. The verbs in David's songs tell this story. They are always about something happening! Seeking, looking, joining, holding, trusting, following - always coming together with one another and with God. Hope is found not just at the destination, but along and with the Way who is Jesus Christ. I'm delighted that David has included his online blog musings about his music in this book - they are all about being on the way.

I hope that in this music you find a gentle hope in God's constant love which meets us in and beyond our sorrows. May you and your community experience the solace of such unbounded grace.

Craig Mitchell

songs

Songs have stayed with me through the long, wrenching coronavirus season.

Songs. Songs as I would never have expected. Lament songs mostly. Songs pouring out of me.

Songs which basically came out of the blue; mostly from dark or at least shady places. Poured out as never before from this eight-songs-a-year writer who's been honing, sharing, stumbling, rejoicing through this songwriting craft for over 45 years.

Songs. Well, strictly speaking mostly *not* songs. By definition, a song is something you sing. It's a poem set to music; musical and lyrical phrases as one. Yes, I wrote plenty of true songs in this season – songs that bounce from lament to gratitude and usually back to lament.

Tunes, melodies, musical phrases - all of them journalling how life has been for me at a particular point in the pandemic journey that has stricken the world in 2020 and no doubt, way beyond. More often than not, however, often in the wee hours of the autumn and winter mornings, a song without words came to me. I say "came" because often I'd be asleep, or at least close to it.

Not only would I be struggling to make meaning of this long season, I'd be struggling to find words to articulate how I was faring. Without doubt the most reflective time in my life.

So, all these instrumentals started pouring out of me. I'd head to my study as dawn was breaking, open up Logic Pro X on my Mac and record that song.

That song without words. Somehow, the song without words was still somehow a song. I'd play the song again and again to myself; almost as therapy, certainly as prayer. Words and thoughts would from time to time reveal themselves. Sometimes not. Yet, words, thoughts, emotion; some I could name, many I could not. Invariably, one-word titles: LOSS, SACRIFICE, CRAZY! More.

I'd post each one on Facebook and my blog. By grace, I'd find them speaking into the hearts, minds and struggles of people everywhere. People half a world away would play the music scores at home … perhaps at their own time and timing. Adding their own life nuances. Somehow, blessing was going back and forth. I'd record those songs – the instrumentals always on piano. Sometimes with some guitar or flute added. Occasional percussion. For most recordings, I stayed with the first take. I didn't want perfection. I wanted to put the songs down there and then. Once again, as I was faring there and then. Raw.

This collection is dedicated to my life-partner for the past 40 years – Dale MacGregor, who through this long pandemic journey has shown the fruits of the Holy Spirit, especially love and patience in beautiful measure.

David MacGregor October 2020

4 March 2020   I'll Hold You Forever (Do Not Fear)

Wanted to post this, and trusting in understanding from my friends not of Christian faith. While at Galveston, Texas, USA just two weeks ago I found myself reflecting on those words found so they say, 365 times in Christian scripture: "Do Not Fear" (or "Do not be afraid") ...

So on GarageBand on my trusty iPad, I wrote this song - "I'll Hold You Forever (Do Not Fear)". I didn't write it with COVID-19 in mind, perhaps this can be my offering to the wider community amid what a long-time mentor would call "strange and interesting times"; indeed so for our world.

This song offers a hope that is beyond us but through faith, as close as. Dale has just put down a wonderful vocal with lovely harmony in the chorus.

> No matter what's around the corner No matter the disorder
> No matter what the danger, You are there
> When worry makes you fear tomorrow
> Not much joy and too much sorrow
> When noises press - come follow
> You are there
>
>> "Do not fear, do not fear
>> I'll hold you in my mercy, I am here
>> I'll be your light - your safest keeping
>> I'll hold you forever, I'll hold you forever
>> I'll hold you forever in my love"
>
> Oh may I seek your life, your kingdom
> Oh may I live your wisdom
> Oh may I walk your freedom every day
> To wait with joy to greet tomorrow
> Find peace in You I'll follow
> through every high or hollow, come what may
>
>> "Do not fear, do not fear ...`

mp3 or YouTube video of this song available at:
https://togethertocelebrate.com.au/songs-of-solace-and-sorrow

David MacGregor © 2020. Willow Publishing

26 March 2020   We've Lit a Candle

A reflective song for you. Today on Facebook, an old friend posted that this day the churches in Scotland have called for a National Day of Prayer in response to COVID-19. Part of this would be for folk at 7 pm to place a lit candle in their home's front window and with that say a prepared prayer.

Bruce Johnson invited folk to do the same and join with him in prayer, hope and solidarity.

So Dale and I did.
Alongside that I found myself reflecting in the writing of a new song - "We've Lit a Candle", the lyrics closely-inspired by those deep Scottish words Bruce posted.

Blessings all ... and thanks again, Bruce.
Maybe a vocal from Dale tomorrow, We'll see

mp3 or YouTube video of this song available at:
https://togethertocelebrate.com.au/songs-of-solace-and-sorrow

We've lit a candle
We've come together
Though separated
we're joined in Love
The way illumined
Your Word is opened
We've brought thanksgiving
for kindness shown.

We light a candle
For the defenseless
For all so anxious
… who fall apart
who need Love's comfort
from deepest sadness
May all their ailing
have healing come

We'll light a candle
In evening's window
For all who lead us
through this long storm
Lord bless and guide us
We live in new ways
May love for neighbour
"rhythm" our hearts.

We'll light a candle
We'll look in hope for
we are your people
who know your Light
May light there shining
know living radiance
in hearts, hands, hoping
through Christ our Lord

David & Dale MacGregor
© 2020 Willow Publishing

This page is left blank to assist in the playing of the piano pieces in this collection.

30 March 2020 — **Fall**

Musing on these times and this season (autumn in southern hemisphere) and all that can and cannot be, this tune came to me. I've called it FALL.

"Fall" seems an apt thought as I reflect on things just weeks into the start of COVID19 restrictions. Who knows where this will lead but it's far from optimistic. Frankly, it's sobering and terrifying.

Well-being, employment, freedoms, confidence and so much more is starting to feel in some way that thing called brokenness. The uncertainty around where all of this heading has this crashing sensation.

I know I'm experiencing it; and I'm in a privileged position of it-would-seem secure employment for starters.

To think that it's under a month and I was walking the seashore at Galveston on the Gulf of Mexico. No trouble with dining, with travel, with movement, with gathering with people.

Things are falling and it's not looking good.
Take care, folks.

mp3 or YouTube video of this song available at:
https://togethertocelebrate.com.au/songs-of-solace-and-sorrow

fall

This page is left blank to assist in the playing of the piano pieces in this collection.

31 March 2020 — **Presence**

We're all differently acclimatising. All differently struggling (if you're not, great!!).

I often find instrumental music works best for me in times like these, amid being a songwriter myself and lover of music with deep, engaging lyrics. Having words around me clutters my headspace.

Those "engaging lyrics" work one of two ways for me. They're very wording evokes all sorts of thoughts and feelings out of my head and heart. They act as a catalyst to give expression to how I'm feeling. The Bible's book of Psalms often do that for me. Plenty of other people too – for thousands of years.

On the other hand, they can easily suppress the emotions and ideas that need release from deep within me. To keep them inside, I know from experience can do unhelpful things with my well-being.

I wrote a piece called FALL just yesterday.
This morning I was prompted to again play an instrumental piece of mine from the early 2000s called **PRESENCE**. It helped me when I played it again.

Maybe it'll support you in some way. Take care.

mp3 or YouTube video of this song available at:
https://togethertocelebrate.com.au/songs-of-solace-and-sorrow

presence

David MacGregor
© 2013

This page is left blank to assist in the playing of the piano pieces in this collection.

3 April 2020   The Long Road

Bob Dylan is on his "Never Ending Tour" which some say began in the mid 1970s!
45 years ago!

He's not currently touring because of COVID. Otherwise Dylan and his trusty band would year in, year out be still at it – a never-ending tour.

As "prompted", I've been writing some simple piano pieces ... my response to where I'm at (and often where the world is at) with this coronavirus pandemic. Who knows how many pieces this suite will have? God forbid, NOT 45 years' worth!

Anyhow, I'm more and more hearing the Australian PM and other politicians & medics talking about us being in for the long haul. Press conferences and media releases many times during the week. Hence this not-terribly-upbeat piece called THE LONG ROAD.

Long haul indeed.
Long haul indeed.

Take care.

mp3 or YouTube video of this song available at:
https://togethertocelebrate.com.au/songs-of-solace-and-sorrow

The Long Road

David MacGregor © 2020 Willow Publishing

6 April 2020   **Be Still**

Psalm 46 is undeniably one of the great psalms of the faith. It begins with these words.

> God is our refuge and strength,
> an ever-present help in trouble.

Fast forward to verse 10 and you have the psalmist's memorable words …
He says, "Be still, and know that I am God;

Many a time … right up to last night, as something quite disturbing was troubling me and I struggled to get to sleep, God's reassuring words came once again to me. I said them prayerfully over and over: Be still and know that I am God. I sang them … finding myself reworking a short chant-like song I wrote a few years back called BE STILL.

Somehow version 1 didn't have enough "still"; enough "know".
It needed to be slower. So here is the new version, Dale providing quite intentionally a subdued background vocal .. .. with a hint of harmony here and there.

> Be still
> Be still
> Be still and know … I am God

mp3 or YouTube video of this song available at:
https://togethertocelebrate.com.au/songs-of-solace-and-sorrow

words: Psalm 46:10 music: David MacGregor © 2020 Willow Publishing

Be Still

♩=110 from Psalm 46:10 music: © David MacGregor 2020

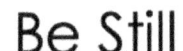

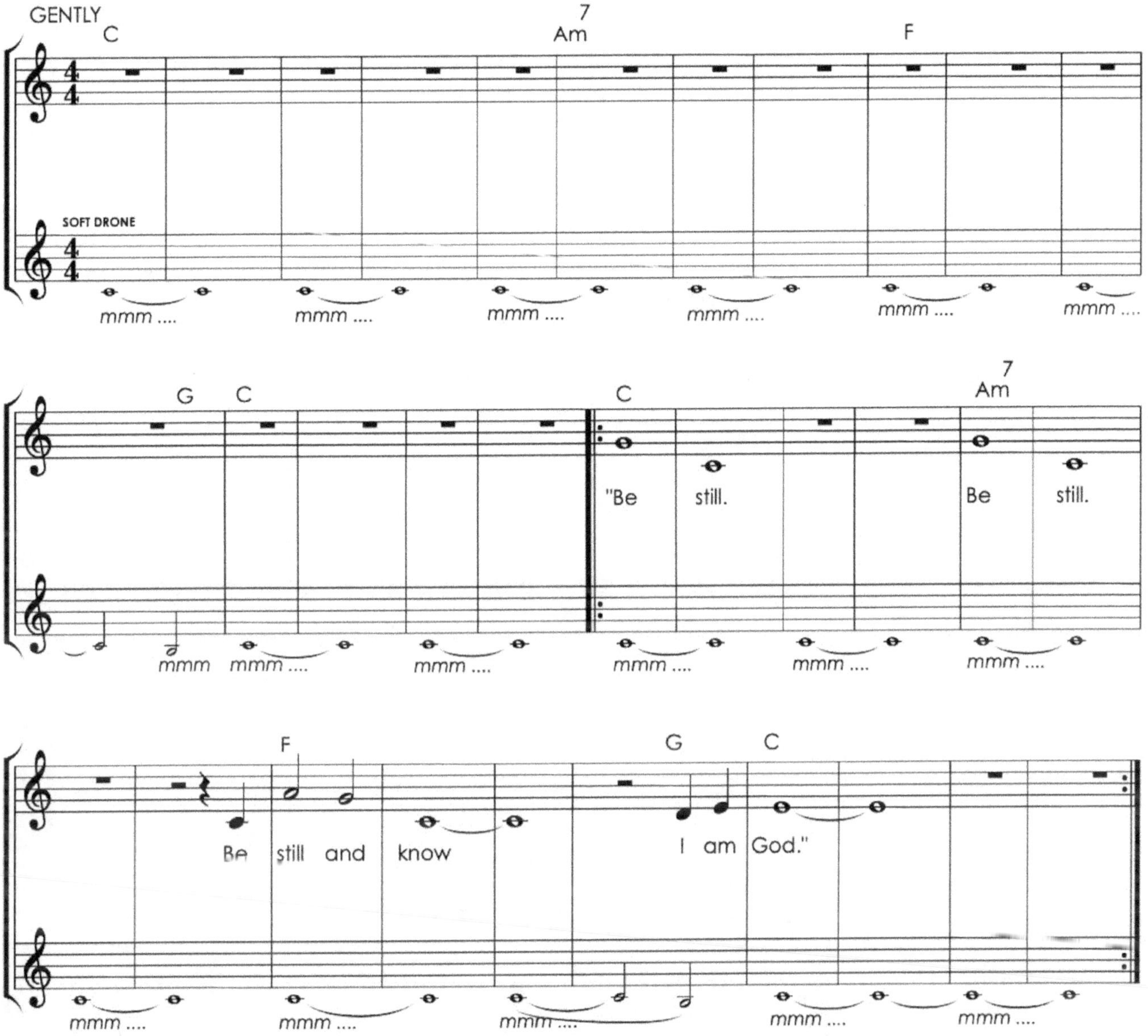

This page is left blank to assist in the playing of the piano pieces in this collection.

7 April 2020   Resilience

Songwriting, especially the instrumental kind is my journaling in these times (and not only these times) ... we're still in the early part of this season.

I've shared a range of reflective pieces so far ... kind of expressing how I'm 'travelling' and those around me ... indeed our world too.

I guess, piece by piece, they're becoming a musical suite. This one's called **RESILIENCE.**

Looking back on my life, I believe I've been a resilient, hardy, low maintenance, endurable kind of person; someone who has got through the challenges of life. Not too much pain and heartache along the way. This pandemic season has certainly shaken me. Of course, probably anyone reading this. The world's – humankind's resilience has been rocked to the core.

Resilience. The tree in the video seems to have mastered that.
Maybe it's something to do with its reaching both up down.
Down to its foundations; to its roots, to all that holds it together in place.
Up to the light. Always upwards and outwards to the light.

I've still got a way to go.

> mp3 or YouTube video of this song available at:
> https://togethertocelebrate.com.au/songs-of-solace-and-sorrow

resilience

David MacGregor © 2020 Willow Publishing

10 April 2020   Sacrifice

Today and tomorrow ... a time for reflection ... remembering sacrifice 2000 years ago ... sacrifices being made in today's COVID-19 times.

Yet, as I write this, I'm ever-mindful in this Easter season, that "sacrifice" is tangible. I'm reminded through the media that around the world, including my own community, people are sacrificing amid this pandemic.

I think of "essential services" workers, especially healthcare and social workers. I think of politicians of all persuasions whose workload has increased so much, along with the pressures of these times.

I think of the so-many who find themselves working from home, sacrificing in many ways the focus they could offer their work.

Now, as I know from folk in my church, there are those who somehow need to balance their work with the needs of parenting young children. There are only so many hours in the day, only so much energy and patience that each of us have.

I think of those who so sadly have sacrificed their job, probably having no say at all in the matter. Mind you their boss probably didn't either.

Are all of these sacrifices predicated on the sacrificial, atoning work of Christ on the cross?

No, but they are sacrifices all the same: humble, selfless and demanding.

So, this piece is simply called: **SACRIFICE**

mp3 or YouTube video of this song available at:
https://togethertocelebrate.com.au/songs-of-solace-and-sorrow

13 April 2020   **Awaken**

My piano-piece writing continues as does the COVID-19 journey we're all on.

This one's an upbeat thing for a change - a bit Celtic/Irish. It would work well with a band! It's called AWAKEN ... informed by the Easter season we're now in, as well as seeing so many people out walking this morning, smiles on faces, in more ways than one, putting their best foot forward ... awakening to possibilities.

If you're like me – and who knows how many are and aren't, you're starting to experience all manner of false dawns. You wake up one morning, the sun is shining – literally and in other ways – and you're up to embracing the new day with all of its possibilities.

Yet the next morning, even if the sun shines, it's so different. For me, the melancholy side of me which has come to the fore in not-so-grand measure in these days presents itself.

Do you know what that's like. I'm guessing you probably do. If you don't, well done!

Still, for me there remains a sense of awakening here, there and everywhere.

Trouble is: will it last?

mp3 or YouTube video of this song available at:
https://togethertocelebrate.com.au/songs-of-solace-and-sorrow

18 April 2020   **Crazy!**

Hi. My latest piece of instrumental music for these COVID-19 times as I/we travel through this season. Not sure if I'm adjusting that brilliantly. Mind you; are any of us? I was going to call this very jazzy piece "Stir Crazy". Sometimes I feel a bit like that. Introvert and home-body that I am, nevertheless (usually with Dale), I love:

- going to the beach for a walk
- having a Southbank or Springfield Orion Lagoon swim
- enjoying a coffee or meal at a local cafe
- going to a movie or play OR the cricket OR football
- worshipping with my church community in person 😀
- having people over when we want to
- travelling

Can't do that right now. None of us can really. We will get through this … I remind myself. My Christian faith reminds me to be still and know God's presence. I keep coming back to Psalm 46:10.

So … with no disrespect to the Willie Nelson/Patsy Cline classic, I'm simply calling this one: CRAZY.

Over 20 years ago while in Cairns, Dale and I wrote an all-ages musical called Scary Times. This coronavirus thing sure is scary … when you consider its implications. "Crazy" is equally apt. So, take a listen. I had some fun putting the recording of this together! Do what you like with it. Loop it and even have a dance.

Some already have!

mp3 or YouTube video of this song available at:
https://togethertocelebrate.com.au/songs-of-solace-and-sorrow

This page is left blank to assist in the playing of the piano pieces in this collection.

22 April 2020   **agitated**

AGITATED.
That's my new piece.

Sums up where I'm at right now.

dictionary.com explains the word as "*adjective. excited; disturbed.*"

Excited? Are you serious?
Disturbed? Absolutely.

More like these synonyms from the same redoubtable website:

flustered
moved
upset

I'm adding a few of my own:

unsettled
restless
uncertain
on edge

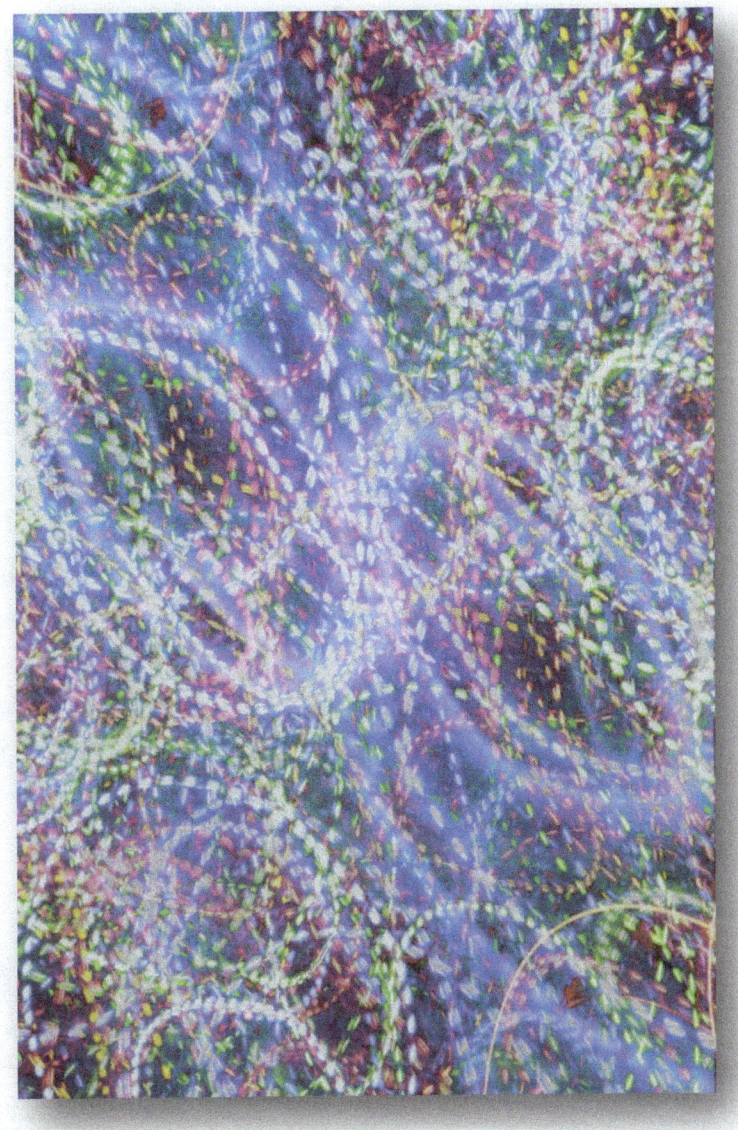

Why?
I guess it's because the reality and potentiality of this COVID19 coronavirus pandemic is really starting to sink in. The news channels devote most of their morning or nightly bulletins to it. Graphs, tables, estimates – all of it so gloomy.

It starts to mess with your head. Starts to mess with your heart, your spirit, your sense of well-being. Politicians and health experts comment how it's going to get a whole lot worse before it starts getting better. There's talk about lockdowns. People are dying. Horror stories coming out of nursing homes and aged care centres.

It's already a month since all in-person activities in my church here in Brisbane were suspended. Who knows how long that will last? I suspect a long time. It's only a month, but I'm missing being part of gathered worship. I've already conducted a funeral for a loved church member … and it's really tough not being able to touch. "Social distancing" is the buzz and necessary word.

Yes – I'm getting more and more agitated. Finding it hard to relax. Agitated.

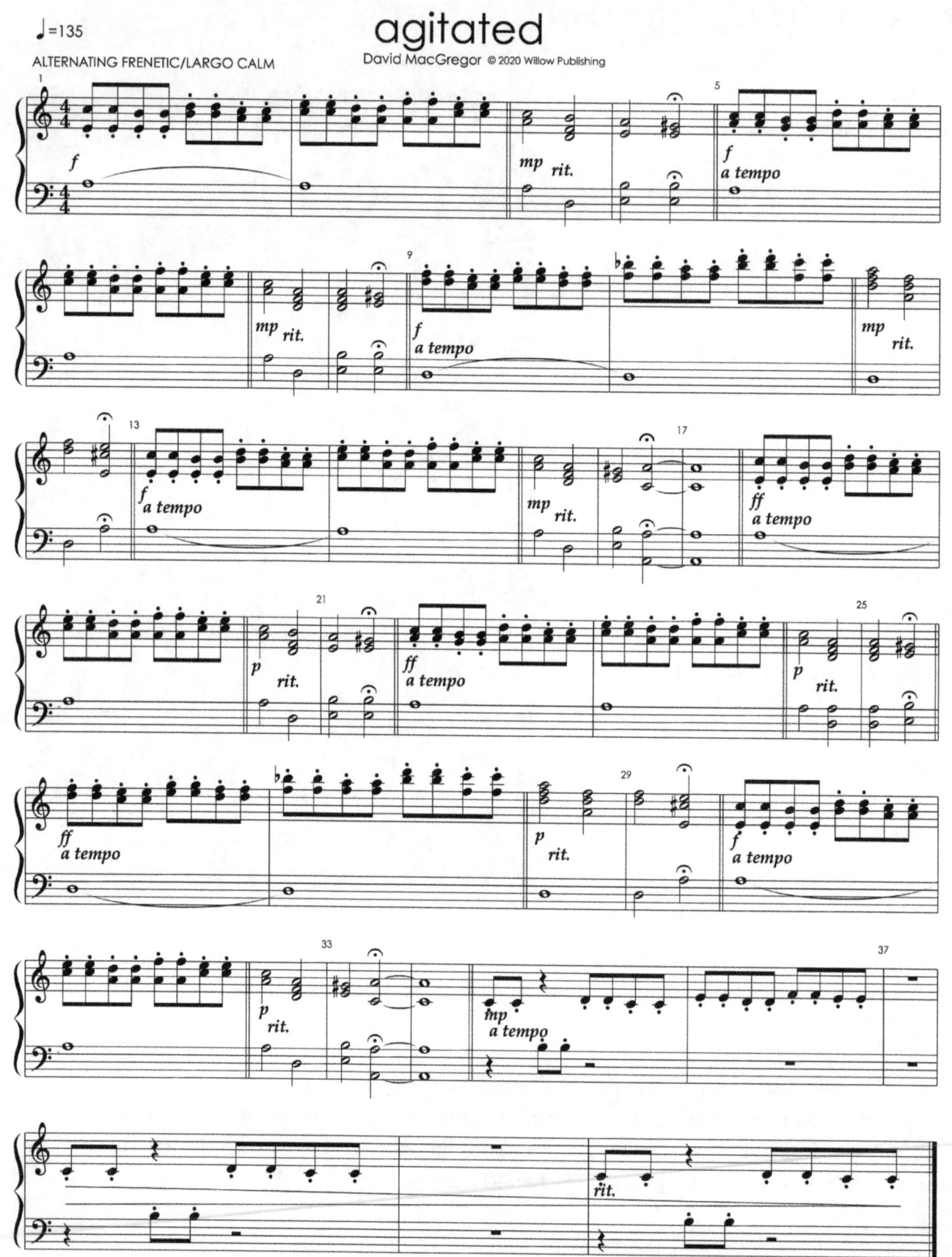

27 April 2020   We will remember them

I really should blog before I Facebook-post. So, I'm playing catch-up and sharing something I wrote three days ago – Anzac Day in Australia and New Zealand; that day when we stand as one and remember all who offered themselves in service for their country … amid the horrors of war and loss of life … down the decades and indeed centuries in many countries.

Actually, the embryo of a song was birthed it the evening before Anzac Day. I couldn't get to sleep. Those memorable words by Laurence Binyon known as "The Ode" wouldn't leave me. I eventually dozed off, but the tune that was forming was still there, through to the morning.

> They shall not grow old, as we that are left grow old
> Age shall not weary them, nor the years condemn
> At the going down of the sun and in the morning
> We will remember them.

Dale and I, Joel's partner Upasana and some neighbours gathered to light up the dawn on our footpath at 6 am, sharing conversation- all socially-distanced and Dale's yummy Anzac biscuits afterwards.

I came in for a while, had a coffee from our new machine, sat some more … then headed into the study. My setting for Binyon's words soon followed. Quite deliberately, apart from repeating the final line, I have not tinkered with these almost-sacred words.

Three generations:
David, Thomas & Howard MacGregor

This setting is in honour of my grandfather, Thomas Laur MacGregor – ambulance officer at Gallipoli, Western Front and the Middle East during WW1.

This page is left blank to assist in the playing of the piano pieces in this collection.

2 May 2020   **Emerging**

My latest piano piece as we journey through this COVID-19 season is **EMERGING**

Dale and I and our friend Upasana had a picnic breakfast this morning at the local Toohey Forest Park, one of our favourite spots.

So nice.

So ... with a few restrictions lifted, I felt inspired to write this piece.

Stay safe and well, folks.

mp3 or YouTube video of this song available at:
https://togethertocelebrate.com.au/songs-of-solace-and-sorrow

This page is left blank to assist in the playing of the piano pieces in this collection.

9 May 2020   Easing

A day after COVID-19 restrictions here in Australia begin to be gradually and carefully lifted, 3+ stages along the way, here's the latest instalment in my journeying/journalling piano suite.

This one's called **EASING.**

This easing sure makes a difference.

Dale and I can now travel not only beyond our neighbourhood, not only up to 50 kilometres.

We can go to the beach. The beach has long been one of our "go to" places. Nothing beats a beach walk to soothe the soul and revive the spirits.

Now we can at last.go to our favourite Snapper Rocks at the southern Gold Coast, take that beach walk, enjoy that coffee and sit at that picnic table, with no fear of the police looking unfavourably at our exploits!!

It's just good to get out and about, smell the flowers, take in the fresh air, and of course - a coffee.

mp3 or YouTube video of this song available at:
https://togethertocelebrate.com.au/songs-of-solace-and-sorrow

easing

10 May 2020 Stitch a new garment

I've just written another song – with words this time. It comes out of both this ongoing coronavirus season and a challenging, insightful, hopeful quote from American poet, humanitarian and activist Sonya Renee Taylor.

> "We will not go back to normal. Normal never was. Our pre-corona existence was never normal other than we normalized greed, inequity, exhaustion, depletion, extraction, disconnection, confusion, rage, hoarding, hate and lack. We should not long to return, My friends. We are being given the opportunity to stitch a new garment. One that fits all of humanity and nature."

I found it on Facebook last weekend. Something started stirring deep within me. For weeks Dale, I and others in my networks has mused over what "normal" would look like once most of the COVID-19 restrictions were lifted.

Who knows? What is clear is that with the world in lockdown or isolation in some way, we have this God-given opportunity to establish new, better, more-compassionate foundations. If you like – a huge reset. I keep on coming back to Jesus' kingdom of God preaching in chapters 5-7 of the Gospel of Matthew.

The clincher was those words from Taylor.

We are being given the opportunity to stitch a new garment.

Wow! A song was soon born: STITCH A NEW GARMENT.

Yesterday, Dale kindly added her vocals. I'm my strongest critic but I'm really happy with how I've preserved (I believe) the integrity of Taylor's quote while adding my "garment" lyricism in the chorus.

See what you think. Yet don't just think, act!

STITCH A NEW GARMENT.

We will not go back to normal
'Cos normal never was
We've done so much reflecting
'bout how life is and was
For normal meant bein' greedy,
meant lack, injustice, rage
Normal meant confusion
Unkindness in our age

> Time to stitch a new garment
> With love in every seam
> Weave in understanding
> That's lived much more than dreamed
> Each colour bein' woven
> in unity, in peace
> Building tomorrow
> May our striving ,
> may our praying
> May our caring never cease

O God give us new hope for
this moment and these times
to weave those deep connections.
God gave this gift of time
to weave a new humanity
through this bewild'ring world
Let's weave in all our colours
that love be lived and shared

> Time to stitch a new garment …

mp3 or YouTube video of this song available at:
https://togethertocelebrate.com.au/songs-of-solace-and-sorrow

David & Dale MacGregor
© 2020 … based on words by Sonya Renee Taylor

14 May 2020   **Perspective**

Just written my 10th instrumental piece in this suite for the season. Earlier this morning I once again found myself immersed in some musical journalling. This time I'm reflecting on a much better past few days.

I've called this one PERSPECTIVE.

It's amazing how doing something as simple as an early morning walk, then grabbing a takeaway breakfast – I'm friends with a noted Scottish fast food clan – then going to a local park under brilliant autumn skies – sunshine, fresh air, you name it, even a bit of a gentle breeze; it sure helps give some perspective on things.   I ask myself: David, "Why aren't you doing this more often?"

It helps you! It lifts your spirits. Again, it gives you some fresh perspective!

I find myself reminded of Psalm 43:1

> Why, my soul, are you downcast? Why so disturbed within me? Put your hope in God, for I will yet praise him, my Saviour and my God.

mp3 or YouTube video of this song available at:
https://togethertocelebrate.com.au/songs-of-solace-and-sorrow

19 May 2020   **liminal**

Some years back, on a ministry retreat, I first heard the words "liminal space". Back then, I "got it"; but not really. I'm a slow learner sometimes, perhaps more than I readily acknowledge. Perhaps I'm just stubborn. Anyway, as I was preparing the second episode in my church's new Midweek Musing last Tuesday – reflecting what a "reset" for both the world and us personally might look like, and continuing to be touched by Sonya Renee Taylor's words (which with Dale I adapted into a recent song: "Stitch a New Garment"), it finally clicked what liminal space was and is.

Liminal space? The word liminal comes from the Latin word 'limen', meaning threshold – any point or place of entering or beginning. A liminal space is the time between the 'what was' and the 'next.' It is a place of transition, a season of waiting, and not knowing. One writer explains liminal space like this: "Liminal space is where all transformation takes place, if we learn to wait and let it form us.

Or , in the words of Richard Rohr, "The threshold is God's waiting room." I like that. Right now, me, you, whoever we are; we are in Gods waiting room.

Now that I'd "got it" (well … have I really … and I suspect, it's more a case of accepting it and as Rohr says, waiting in it), I wrote another piano piece: **LIMINAL.**

> mp3 or YouTube video of this song available at:
> https://togethertocelebrate.com.au/songs-of-solace-and-sorrow

liminal

David MacGregor © 2020   Willow Publishing

26 May 2020   Your love will follow

Amid these up and down times for us, there are constants. I've mused much about "what sustains us".

The love of Dale and others sustains me. So does scripture. So does music. So does the beauty of God's creation – especially beach and bush. I could say coffee too.

The love, presence of God and God's prevenient grace sustains me especially – on the bad days, the good and the in-between. Prevenient Grace is a term I discovered almost 30 years ago, as I began my involvement in the Walk to Emmaus movement. It's a term coined by John Wesley as he mused on the dimensions of God's grace in Christ. Prevenient grace is grace that woos us, seeks us out, follows us, is ever-present; never lets us go. Through all of the past many months of change, lockdown, rearrangement and realignment and so much more, I've never lost sight of that.

Through a song by New Zealand writer and friend Malcolm Gordon, I've recently been reacquainted with that middle-ages piece known down the centuries as St Patrick's Breastplate. It's much longer than this, but lines from it such as these kept ringing in my head:

Christ, be with me, Christ before me, Z
Christ behind me,
Christ in me, Christ beneath me, Christ above me,
Christ on my right, Christ on my left,
Christ where I lie, Christ where I sit,

mp3 or YouTube video of this song available at:
https://togethertocelebrate.com.au/songs-of-solace-and-sorrow

In the wee hours of this morning, this somewhat-hymn-like song came to me:

YOUR LOVE WILL FOLLOW

Strength to guide and wisdom deep
Lord, your love will follow
Your ear to hear, your word to speak
Lord, your love will follow
Hand to guard, and way to walk
Lord, your love will follow
You are faith and hope and love
Lord, your love
Lord, your love will follow.

Before, behind, around me Lord
With us now, forever
Within, beside, above me Lord
With us now, forever
When I rise and when I rest
With us now, forever
You are faith and hope and love
With us nowWith us now, forever

Comforter and Spirit-friend
God, your presence always
In my highs and in my lows
God, your presence always
Christ my hope and Christ my life
God, your presence always
You are faith and hope and love
Lord, your love
With us now
God, your presence always

David MacGregor
© 2020 Willow Publishing
inspired by portions of
"St Patrick's Breastplate

29 May 2020 — Make it joyful!

I don't write many praise songs. I've often wondered down the years why this is. Is it because I'm less than praiseworthy in my spirit, somehow lacking in my adoration of God? Maybe. Is it because of my longstanding restlessness about the way so many churches seem to base so much of their musical repertoire on songs of praise and avoid (or at least fail to recognise) the place of songs of lament, confession, mission, justice, discipleship, community, and so on? Maybe.

Amid this strange and tragic pandemic season, the melancholy side of me has certainly come to the fore. That's me. That's life. That's been my journey, which I've shared in song, patient that you are😄

However, I found myself woken in the early hours of the morning yesterday with my namesake's wonderful words from Psalm 100. Yes, I was surprised. A praise song at 2 am?. Sleepy-eyed … wanting so, so much to get back to sleep, I took my iPhone and noted the chorus words and with a series of hieroglyphics made sure I'd remember the melody. As it turned out, I actually remembered it when I woke later. Always a good sign! It's one of the least syncopated songs I've written for a long, long time -unusual for me . Anyhow here's my new song of praise: MAKE IT JOYFUL! Hopefully I have.

>   Make a joyful noise to God (make it joyful)
>   Make a joyful noise to God (make it joyful)
>   Make a joyful noise to God (make it joyful)
>   Come worship and be glad!
>
>   Come before him with praise, thanksgiving
>   God has made us and we are God's
>   We are God's people embraced in love
>   Come bless, come bless the Lord
>
>   Make a joyful noise to God (make it joyful) …
>
>   For the Lord is every goodness
>   And God's love is steadfast, sure
>   From generation to generation
>   God's faithfulness endures
>
>   Make a joyful noise to God (make it joyful) …
>   … Come worship and be glad! (make it joyful)
>   Come worship and be glad !(make it joyful)
>   Come worship and be glad! (make it joyful)

> mp3 or YouTube video of this song available at:
> https://togethertocelebrate.com.au/songs-of-solace-and-sorrow

David MacGregor © 2020 Willow Publishing – from Psalm 100

Make It Joyful!

David MacGregor © 2020 Willow Publishing

based on Psalm 100

♩.=60
WITH AN UPBEAT LILT, STRONG 1st BEAT

This page is left blank to assist in the playing of the piano pieces in this collection.

19 June 2020   Image of LOVE

For some time I've found myself pondering what the Christian and Jewish faiths (others too?) are saying when they affirm we human creatures are mind-blowingly made … created in the image of God; or as some would express it, in God's likeness. Christian thinkers use the Latin words imago dei when talking about this.

Events recently in the USA of racism and sparked by racism … not only there but the history of treatment of First People's in our own country have spurred on this pondering.

Imago dei … image of God. What does this all mean? What are the implications, the responsibilities of believing this? In the Bible's first creation narrative, we read:

> Then God said, "Let us make humankind in our image, according to our likeness; and let them have dominion over the fish of the sea, and over the birds of the air, and over the cattle, and over all the wild animals of the earth, and over every creeping thing that creeps upon the earth." So God created humankind in his image, in the image of God he created them; male and female he created them. Genesis 1:26-27 NRSV

Doesn't get much clearer than that. Yet, if we are like God, what/who is God like?! We can only unpack that in human terms and from human experience.

I read from this, as evidenced throughout the scriptures and ultimately in Jesus Christ, that if we understand and know God as God of love, justice, mercy, welcome, hospitality, hope, inclusion, presence and salvation … we of faith are likewise (and likewise sure is the word) to be people of love, justice, mercy, welcome, hospitality, hope, inclusion, presence and salvation.

Is this simply a no-brainer? I wish it was. Sadly, our human condition so, so distorts the image or likeness of God we are made to be. We are created in God's likeness but our lives and the life of the world point to other images – images and experiences of decay, ignorance, oppression, hate, harm, loss, injustice, environmental and human pillage … it's that word sin.

Actually, we cannot affirm that we, by God's Grace are made in God's image, without in turn realising how this will impact (& indeed needs to) so much of how we go about life, in fact all of our lives.

Has our image of God become so distorted that it sanctions excluding certain people from being image bearers? Are we representing God to people in a way that contributes to their devaluing others?

The race riots, demonstrations (mostly peaceful we need reminding) and the police brutality that served as catalyst for it, forces us to ask: not just how I see my neighbour … who is the other person to me? Does my faith lead me again and again back, back to the affirmation that they too are created in the image, potential and goodness of God.

When we fail to attend with compassion towards the hungry, the thirsty, the naked, the stranger, the imprisoned … we fail to attend to no less than God … to the one in whose image the hungry, the thirsty, the naked, the stranger, the imprisoned are made.

God gives us a clear choice … by our words, by our hands, by our hearts and so much more we can incredibly bless others … incredibly bless others OR we can do something so opposite to that, that pains God … that pains another made also, just as we are, in the imago dei … the image of God.

So, with all this occupying my mind. My heart, my spirit, I found myself writing a little song … wanting to use a simplicity of lyrics.

I've called it **IMAGE OF LOVE**

> Made in the image
> Made in the image
> Made in the image of God
> Created with promise
> With hope and with wonder
> Made in the image of Love
>
> Reflecting the holy
> Reflecting the holy
> Reflecting your holiness, God
> Created with promise
> With hope and with wonder
> Reflecting your holiness, God
>
> Seeing in the other
> Seeing in the other
> the hand of our God in each one
> Created with promise
> With hope and with wonder
> each made in the image of Love
>
> (Hummed)
> Mmm …
> Mmm …
> Mmm …
> Created with promise
> With hope and with wonder
> May we be your image of Love
> May we be your image of Love
> May we be your image of Love

mp3 or YouTube video of this song available at:
https://togethertocelebrate.com.au/songs-of-solace-and-sorrow

David MacGregor © 2020 Willow Publishing

8 July 2020   Lord, how we thank you

I can only put it down to being a "God thing" but here I am, mid 60's, less than eight months to retirement, have written 400+ songs in my lifetime … and I'm suddenly writing praise songs. 99% of that 400+ have not been praise songs. My previous song a month ago: *Make it Joyful!* was a praise song too. What's happening here?! Why's it taken so long. Has the pandemic journey I've been on (i.e. we've all been on) drawn something new out of me, alongside affecting me deeply. I guess it's a bit of both. So here's a new song: **LORD, HOW WE THANK YOU.**

In the last week or so I've been reminded again and again about not only the place but the necessity of gratitude – showing our thanks, showing how grateful we are for all that's good, refreshing and life giving for us.

This COVID-19 season has had its moments for all of us … I'm no exception. I've found myself melancholic again and again these past months. Yes, I've had my up times, let's be clear, but I've had my share of down times … my well-being and most likely yours has been impacted.

Quite unexpectedly, the songwriter in me has found myself journalling through this crazy season … not so much in words but in one short instrumental piece after another. Occasionally a piece with both tune and words. Probably their short titles say it all: FALL, SACRIFICE, CRAZY, RESTLESS, THE LONG ROAD, RESILIENCE …

Then God's Spirit prompted me recently about gratitude.

- When I sat in my front lawn under a sunny blue winter sky, freshly brewed coffee in my hand, I found myself so grateful – thank you God.
- When I walked through that national park, heard the sounds of bush, air and ocean … I found myself so grateful – thank you God.
- When I found myself playing that Indigo Girls song with its exquisite harmonies over and over again … I found myself so grateful – thank you God.
- When Dale and I shared four lovely days with special friends from Cairns … I found myself so grateful – thank you God.

- When I found myself in stitches such was the banter in a recent church ministry team meeting … I found myself so grateful – thank you God.
- When I was reminded of God's amazing, faithful, never-ending love for me in Jesus … I found myself so grateful – thank you God.

In the Bible we find verse after verse about gratitude… about thanksgiving …

Give thanks to the Lord, for he is good. God's love endures forever. Psalm 136:1

"Let the peace of Christ rule in your hearts, since as members of one body you were called to peace. And be thankful." Colossians 3:15

Always be joyful and never stop praying. Whatever happens , keep thanking God because of Jesus Christ. This is what God wants you to do.   1 Thessalonians 5:16-18

One catalyst for gratitude for me was a blogpost from noted Lutheran pastor Nadia Bolz-Weber, called "Give Us This Day Our Daily Gratitude". God was able to use that blog for God's purposes in me! Nadia Bolz-Weber writes …

> I swear to God, exercise and gratitude are like, God's own anti-depressants. In this time of loss and suffering and turmoil, when not one of us is spared of sorrow, this morning I made myself list some things I am genuinely grateful for right now, today, in this very moment. And it made me feel better.

So, the song, based closely on scripture has these lyrics:

> Lord, how we thank You
> Lord, how we thank You
> Your mercy, compassion
> it never ends
> We sing out our praises
> Your grace beyond gracious
> Lord, how we thank you
> your boundless love
>
> Love ever steadfast
> Mercy unending
> New every morning
> Your way of love
> Love ever faithful
> calls from me, "grateful"
> Lord, be our worship
> You are our love
>
> Lord, how we thank You. Lord, how we thank You …

mp3 or YouTube video of this song available at:
https://togethertocelebrate.com.au/songs-of-solace-and-sorrow

David MacGREGOR © 2020 Willow Publishing

30 July 2020   **loss**

I have sought to take time out and will continue to do so, but it doesn't erase the sense of loss I so deeply feel. Obviously everyone's context and way-of-dealing-with-things is unique, just as they are unique in God's crafting, but I feel loss in so many ways.

I'm surprised by being able to name many of them, strong introvert that I am

It's the loss of experiencing so many "last" ministry events or services; whether that be the annual ministry retreat which I so look forward to each year, healthy ministry breakfasts just catching up with colleagues from around the place, attending my final synod gathering while in full time ministry, this year's Easter and Pentecost services, my church's annual prayer retreat day.

The loss continues. I'm talking about the loss of any real sense of routine or normality from week to week. It's the loss of weekly preaching opportunities. My weekly online SSUC midweek musing is an attempt to mutually deal with that. Yet I keep naming loss: the loss of regular face to face pastoral ministry with my local church community esp. with seniors, the loss of opportunity in my final year to go to Iona and spend time with the Community there (true: hopefully some time in the future that option might re-emerge).

Loss also with the way Dale and I expected to spend 2020 – Dale in 1st year of post-teaching retirement and me preparing for retirement. Particularly, the loss of feeling of well-being, excitement or joy. I'm so often feeling flat, no energy.

Yet I'm so aware of a few things how countless others near and far are experiencing the loss of loved ones whose hand they couldn't even hold in their final days, the loss of employment and so much more that breaks the heart. Loss. Everyone's loss is unique, tragic. All I can say is that for me; the word, the feeling, the deep paining for me is also ..loss.

So yesterday, I woke up early and the following lament tune "came". Yes, I've called it **LOSS.**

I name it for what it is. I give thanks for my musical gifting … which has enable some totally-unexpected mostly-instrumental journalling and the love of Dale, my family and church family. That has helped, along with God's constant grace fresh every morning.

mp3 or YouTube video of this song available at:
https://togethertocelebrate.com.au/songs-of-solace-and-sorrow

5 August 2020 — Gathering stones together

As a child of the 60s and especially 70s, songs like Pete Seeger's "Turn, Turn, Turn" and particularly the Byrds' classic interpretation of it are indelibly etched deep in the memory banks. Based closely on verses from Ecclesiastes 3:1-8 in the Bible, they speak to the times, that everything has a season. Of course I type this during an ever-lingering pandemic season. Victoria has just recorded a record 725 new COVID-19 cases and Queensland is about to close its borders to New South Wales and the ACT. What "under heaven" is this world coming to?

More than once during this season I've mused how this is a God-given time in birthing a new normal; to come together across the political, cultural, racial, religious and philosophical divides. Yes, come together. Seems so many of my songs use that word – together. I just can't escape it.. We simply mustn't. No apologies … when I read St Paul writing in 2 Corinthians 5 of the call to be reconcilers with one another, thanks to Christ making that possible.

Today I was musing about all of this; the song of course, but particularly that line for Ecclesiastes 3: a time to throw away stones, and a time to gather stones together. That really struck me. Humanly speaking, that's what the world needs. We need to be on about gathering stones together … building on … building up each other. My stone touching yours and yours mine. No time for throwing stones or prejudice or exclusion or oppressive practices or just plain ignorance at another.

So **GATHERING STONES TOGETHER** was birthed. I've stayed close to the Biblical text, rearranging text here and there for purposes of rhyme and emphasis. All the way I've tried reiterating that it's surely time in this new world, this new, strange season to gather stones; stones smooth, rough, big, small, bright, dark together. The Kingdom of God and the love Jesus offers and calls from us demands nothing less.

> Time for everything, time for everything
> Time for everything under heaven
> Time for birth, for dying
> Time for laughing, crying
> Time for gathering stones together, wo-oh-oh
> Time for gathering stones together
>
> Time for love's embrace, time for love's embrace
> Time for everything under heaven
> Time for breaking down
> Time for building up,
> Time for gathering stones together. wo-oh-oh
> Time for gathering stones together

> Time to plant, to reap; to discard, to keep
> Time for everything under heaven
> Time to tear, to sow
> Time to gather, throw
> Time for gathering stones together, wo-oh-oh
> Time for gathering stones together
>
> > Time to come together, wo-oh-oh (x3)
> > Time for gathering stones together …
>
> Time for war, for peace; time to dance, to weep
> Time for everything under heaven
> Time to lose, to seek
> Time for silence, speak.
> Time for gathering stones together, wo-oh-oh
> Time for gathering stones together, wo-oh-oh
> Time for gathering stones together.

mp3 or YouTube video of this song available at:
https://togethertocelebrate.com.au/songs-of-solace-and-sorrow

David MacGregor
© 2020 Willow Publishing from Ecclesiastes 3

19 September 2020   emptying

Our church embarks tomorrow on a four-week journey through Paul's Letter to the Philippians – with a key passage from each chapter.

On the 27th, it's Philippians 2:1-13; a passage which some scholars believe contains fragments from or pointers to a hymn from the early Christian church.

It's one of the great passages in Christian scripture. I actually wrote a song a few years back based on some of these verses. Countless songs have been written down the years connecting with the passage!

However, in browsing the net for some resources, I came across Jan Richardson's wonderful *The Painted Prayerbook* site and a poignant piece of reflection, followed by a blessing; all of it called *Blessing that Becomes Empty*.

It begins with these verses from Philippians:

> Let the same mind be in you that was in Christ Jesus, who, though he was in the form of God, did not regard equality with God as something to be exploited, but emptied himself.   – Philippians 2.5-7a

Then follows the reflection and blessing. Trusting I'm not breaking too much copyright here, I share some of it with you. Jan Richardson's thoughts on "emptying" really resonate with me, and the pandemic well-being journey I've been on and I've shared with many of you via this blog or social media. I reflected how it would work well to have a quite piano instrumental playing behind the blessing, so with the title of **EMPTYING**, I share this with you.

From the pen of Jan Richardson ….

> Encompassed by the Christ who enfolds our emptiness in his own, we become free to choose how we will respond to the emptying. In the emptying that naturally happens in life, as well as in the emptying Christ asks us to seek out and embrace, how will we allow the hollowing to open our hearts to the world we are called to serve in joy and in love?
>
> As you attend to the empty spaces—in your life and in the world—may those spaces open wide to the joy that comes.

mp3 or YouTube video of this song available at:
https://togethertocelebrate.com.au/songs-of-solace-and-sorrow

emptying

David MacGregor © 2020 Willow Publishing

Dear COVID

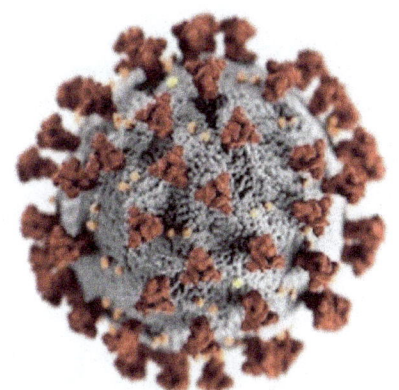

I could write you just so many letters right now.
I could write the letter of lament.

Lament for how in the words of Powderfinger, "These days turned out nothing like I had planned".
Lament for how Dale and I envisioned her first year of retirement blending in with my last in full time ministry, my last with a community who had embraced us and I had embraced likewise for 6 fruitful years, much anticipated retirement study leave at Iona in Scotland, so much, so much

Lament for the loss that's been so much part of this year / loss - yep, that's been such a reality for me - loss in physical & particularly mental well-being. Lament for being unable to be part of helping nurture community in the way I'd hoped.

Lament around this being so much about me. What about the 8 billion others dealing with you, COVID. *COVID you're not my friend.*

Then another letter - a letter of frustration
Frustration over the challenges that various stages of lockdown have presented themselves to me / freedoms I had enjoyed / all sorts of hopes
Frustration over those qualities I had for so long: hopefulness, resilience, stamina, multitasking ... now in short supply. Some ... no more
Frustration with those I've met who think you are one, big overblown hoax, COVID. How does that make you feel, COVID!? *COVID you're not my friend. Actually, COVID are you anyone's friend?*

But COVID, perhaps I could write you a different letter - a letter full of gratitude - and a lot of it's to do with music.
Gratitude for the musical composing journey you've brought from me (a bit of help from God and an encouraging wife too I might add)
Gratitude that over almost 30 songs / mostly piano instrumentals you've brought me into deep reflection. It's been like therapy, COVID. Therapy. Music and more music pouring out of me - blessing others in their time of loss and dislocation - all of an outlet for my soul, my spirit, and *toss in* the Holy Spirit!
Gratitude for being "given" (not by you, COVID, you're not nice like that) - being "given" the gift of time - time to reflect, reassess, to - in the words of a song I was inspired to write, to "stitch a new garment" seeking a new normal of compassion, inclusion, welcome and hope and peace.
Gratitude that amidst this burgeoning suite of musical pieces, I've written a praise song - straight from the psalms. Then another song of thankfulness
Gratitude for the music - mostly the reflective acoustic music you've drawn me to listen to. Here I am amid COVID just loving Taylor Swift's latest: FOLKLORE. Go figure!
Hey COVID, I bet you didn't see that coming! Neither did I!

Three letters I could write you. No doubt there's a fourth and a fifth. No idea. I might hold off sending any of these though. I pray for the day when COVID19, you're done and dusted, no more pain and loss. How good would that be?! Then perhaps I'll send all of this to you ... plus the final paragraph or so. But hey - you're gone. Who's going to read it!?!

David MacGregor   October 2020   Tarragindi, Brisbane, Australia

ISBN 978-0-646-82747-6

www.ingramcontent.com/pod-product-compliance
Lightning Source LLC
Chambersburg PA
CBHW080856230426
43662CB00013B/2121